BODYSCOPE

Movers & Shapers

BODYSCOPE

Movers & Shapers

Bones, muscles and joints

Dr Patricia Macnair

Consultant:

Richard Walker

KINGFISHER

KINGFISHER

Kingfisher Publications Plc,
New Penderel House,
283–288 High Holborn,
London WC1V 7HZ
www.kingfisherpub.com

First published by Kingfisher
Publications Plc 2004
10 9 8 7 6 5 4 3 2 1
1TR/0704/PROSP/PICA(PICA)/140MA/F

ISBN 0 7534 0966 6

A CIP catalogue record for
this book is available from
the British Library.

Printed in China

Copyright © Kingfisher
Publications Plc 2004

Author: Dr Patricia Macnair
Consultant: Richard Walker
Editor: Clive Wilson
Designer: Peter Clayman
Illustrators: Sebastian Quigley, Guy Smith
Picture researcher: Kate Miller
Production controller: Lindsey Scott
DTP coordinator: Jonathan Pledge
Indexer: Sue Lightfoot

Contents

Movement and support

Imagine your body without bones. You would be floppy and unable to move. The bones form a framework, or skeleton, that supports the body and protects the internal organs. Muscles cover the bones. Together, they give the body shape and allow you to move.

► This diver is about to launch herself into the air. Her body is supported by the bones that make up her skeleton.

◄ You need to use over 60 muscles and bones in each hand and arm just to lift a glass.

▲ Hundreds of muscles, of different shapes and sizes, cover the bones.

Pulling power

In order to make a movement, the muscles and bones must work together as a team. When muscles contract, or get shorter, they pull on the bones. This makes different parts of the body change position. Most movements are controlled by the brain.

No rest

Your muscles and bones never stop working. Even when you are standing still, they are busy holding the body in the correct position. And day and night, the muscles and bones in your ribcage are moving to help you breathe.

▶ This picture, called a CT scan, shows the inside of a person's head. The bones of the skull protect the brain. The left-hand side of the brain is not shown in this scan.

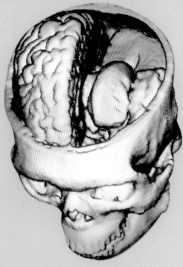

◀ ▼ During the dive, the muscles pull on the bones. This makes the body bend or straighten.

Guard duty

Bones and muscles also have the important job of protecting the organs inside your body. The skull forms a hard box around the brain. Your ribs shield the heart and lungs, and the bones and muscles of the pelvis protect the bladder and organs of reproduction.

infolab

- Bone is stronger than a steel bar of the same weight.

- Over half the bones in your body are found in your hands and feet.

- Muscles are grouped in pairs.

- Muscles make up about half of the weight of your body.

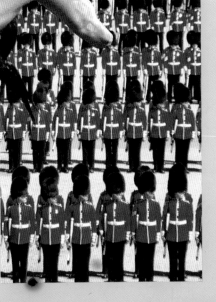

▶ To stand to attention, these soldiers are using muscles in their necks, backs and legs.

Bony framework

The skeleton is made up of bones of all shapes and sizes. Arm and leg bones are long and thin, while hand bones are small and rounded. Although bones are hard and rigid, they can grow and change their shape.

▼ Long bones such as the femur, or thigh bone, are filled with marrow. The blood vessels provide bone cells with food and oxygen.

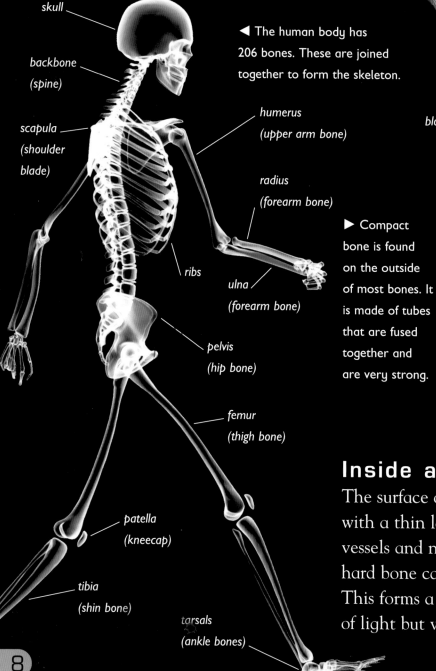

skull

backbone (spine)

scapula (shoulder blade)

ribs

pelvis (hip bone)

femur (thigh bone)

patella (kneecap)

tibia (shin bone)

tarsals (ankle bones)

humerus (upper arm bone)

radius (forearm bone)

ulna (forearm bone)

◄ The human body has 206 bones. These are joined together to form the skeleton.

► Compact bone is found on the outside of most bones. It is made of tubes that are fused together and are very strong.

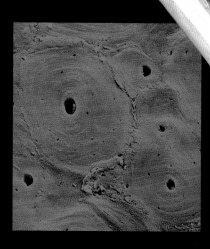

blood vessel

compact bone

spongy bone

Inside a bone

The surface of each bone is covered with a thin layer containing blood vessels and nerves. Underneath is hard bone called compact bone. This forms a shell around a layer of light but very strong spongy bone.

▶ The shape of the skeleton helps the body to balance upright, leaving the hands free. Bones in the feet make a wide base. The pelvis, formed from the hip bones, supports the upper body.

Bone marrow

Spongy bone is packed with jelly-like red bone marrow. This is where blood cells are made. As a child grows into an adult, the red bone marrow in long bones is replaced by yellow bone marrow, which stores fat.

bone marrow

spongy bone

Getting it right

Over time, bones can change their shape because they are made of millions of living cells. This is why it is very important to have your feet measured when you buy shoes. Shoes that are too tight can damage the bones of your feet.

▶ Special scans can detect if the bones of a living person are diseased. This picture shows a healthy skeleton.

▼ Spongy bone is not solid. It is made up of a network of bony struts. The spaces are filled with bone marrow.

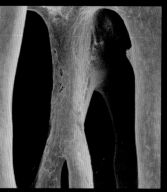

The joints

Wherever two or more bones meet up, you will find a joint. In some joints, the bones are fixed tightly together. In others, the bones can move freely, allowing different parts of the body to bend or twist. Without this flexibility, it would be almost impossible for you to move.

Smooth operators

Joints have to work smoothly to prevent wear and tear. In joints such as the knee, the bone ends have a slippery coating called cartilage. A fluid, in between the layers of cartilage, stops the bones rubbing together.

pelvis
(hip bone)

femur
(thigh bone)

▲ This picture was taken with an endoscope. It shows the cartilage inside a knee joint.

fluid

cartilage

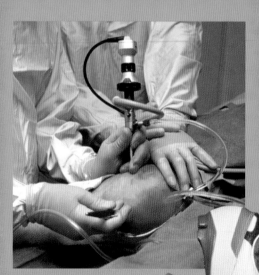

▲ Joints and other parts of the body can be examined by a special instrument called an endoscope.

▲ Two bones meet at the knee, forming a joint. Fluid in the space between the cartilage lets the joint work smoothly.

Chain of bones

Your spine is often called the backbone, but if it was just one rigid bone you would be unable to bend over. Instead, it is made up of many small bones, or vertebrae, with narrow joints in between each of them.

▼ The joints between each vertebra of the spine can move slightly apart.

vertebra

joint

► This x-ray shows a dislocated finger joint, or knuckle. You can see how the two bones have been pushed apart.

Dislocation

Bones are held very tightly in place at the joint by tough bands called ligaments. If a bone is knocked hard enough, it may move out of place. This is called a dislocation, and the joint will not bend properly until the bone is put back into the right place.

How joints move

Joints move in many different ways. Some joints work like a hinge – bend your knee to see this in action. Others, such as the shoulder, let you make movements in most directions.

Ball and socket

Your hip and shoulder are examples of ball and socket joints. One bone rotates just like a ball inside a cup-like socket formed by another bone. Ball and socket joints are the most moveable of all joints.

Hinges and pivots

The knee, elbow, fingers and toes contain hinge joints. These move backwards and forwards in one direction only. The elbow also contains a pivot joint, which lets you turn your hand over and back again.

a ball and socket joint is in each shoulder

the saddle joint is only found in the hand

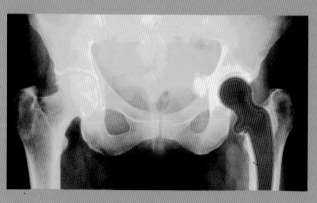

▲ If a hip joint becomes diseased, it can be replaced with an artificial joint made of metal (shown in red).

infolab

■ People with 'double joints' do not have extra joints – they are just more flexible.

■ Every step you take involves the 33 joints in each of your feet.

■ In some of the ankle and wrist joints, the bones glide over each other.

the pivot joint at the top of the spine allows the head to turn

▲ This perfomer can twist and turn her body into this shape because she has very flexible joints.

Thumb power

The saddle joint is found at the base of the thumb. This joint lets you move your thumb in a wide circle. Along with your fingers, your thumb helps you to grip objects in your hand.

in the knee is a hinge joint

Flexibility

Imagine being able to tuck your feet behind your ears! Some people have extremely flexible joints, so they can bend their bodies into unusual and extreme positions.

◄ The body has several different kinds of joints. Each one allows a different movement, from bending the knee to moving the arm in a circle.

Bendy bits

Try folding your ears forwards. They should bend easily and spring back when you let go! This happens because they are made from a flexible tissue called cartilage. Your nose and voicebox, which is the bumpy part in your neck, also contain cartilage.

On the nose

Your nose is made of several pieces of cartilage. They form the sides of your nose and give your nostrils shape. A central piece of cartilage, called the septum, divides the inside of the nose into two chambers.

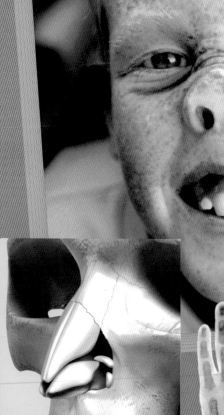

◄ Cartilage is soft enough for an ear to be pierced.

▲ The upper part of the nose is made of hard bone. Plates of cartilage (grey) form the rest of the nose.

cartilage

two-year-old child

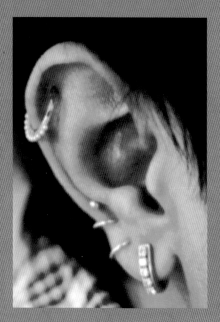

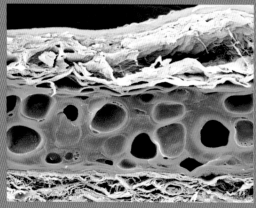

◄ In this picture, taken with a microscope, you can see a layer of cartilage (green) surrounded by skin. The holes contain cells that make cartilage.

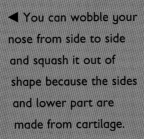

◄ You can wobble your nose from side to side and squash it out of shape because the sides and lower part are made from cartilage.

bone

Soft skeleton

For the first six weeks, a baby developing in its mother's womb has a skeleton made of cartilage. Cartilage is softer and more flexible than bone and allows for rapid growth and change.

bone

◄ These x-rays show a hand at different stages of development. By the time adulthood is reached, the cartilage (lighter areas) has been replaced by bone (blue).

seven-year-old child

adult

Growth and repair

Cartilage is easily damaged, especially in the knee joint. Many athletes have to retire because of cartilage injuries. But scientists are now able to grow new cartilage in the laboratory, giving hope to injured athletes.

Cartilage into bone

In young children, the bones still contain large areas of cartilage in between more rigid bone. These pieces of cartilage are called growth plates, because they let bones grow. Over time, most cartilage is replaced by bone.

Muscles that get you moving

Without muscles you would not be able to scratch your head, open a door or turn a single page of this book! The muscles you use for these and most other movements are joined to the bones. Muscles work by pulling on the bones.

Under the skin

There are almost 650 muscles in your body that you can control and move. This type of muscle, called skeletal muscle, is connected firmly to the bones by tough, string-like cords. These are the tendons.

this muscle wrinkles your forehead

chest muscles pull the arm forwards

this muscle twists the body

the thigh muscle straightens the knee

▶ Underneath your skin are hundreds of overlapping muscles. Most are attached to your skeleton.

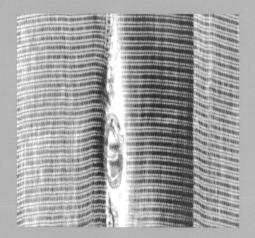

muscle fibres

▲ ▶ Muscle is made from long muscle cells, called fibres, packed together in bundles (right). Under a microscope, these fibres look striped (above).

the trapezius muscle pulls the head and shoulders back

the deltoid muscle raises the arm

the buttock muscle straightens the thigh

the calf muscle bends the foot downwards

How muscles work

Muscles move the body because they are attached to the skeleton. When a muscle contracts, it gets shorter and pulls on a bone. Try bending your arm. If you put your hand on the upper part of the arm, you should feel the muscle become fatter as it gets shorter.

Muscle pairs

The muscles we use for movement are controlled and co-ordinated by the brain. Most muscles work in pairs. One pulls in one direction and the other pulls in the opposite direction.

biceps

◀ ▼ The biceps muscle at the front of the upper arm bends the arm up at the elbow. The triceps, at the back, straightens the arm out.

triceps

17

The skull

The skull is a hard box, made of bone. It contains and protects the brain and other soft parts, such as the eyes, ears and tongue, which can be damaged easily. Nerves and blood vessels go in and out from the brain through holes in the skull.

▲ This decorated skull mask is used during the Mexican Day of the Dead festival. Ancestors are remembered and celebrated on this day.

parietal bone forms the top and side of the skull

Bone head

The skull is formed from 22 bones. Eight of these are large, flat bones that make up a domed box called the cranium. This surrounds the brain. The remaining bones give shape to the face. Only one skull bone can move – the jaw bone, or mandible.

▲ An exploded view of the skull shows how the bones fit together like a jigsaw. The jagged edges lock the bones into place.

▲ This cyclist is taking no chances. A helmet protects his skull and brain from knocks and blows.

Balancing act

The bones of the cranium fit together very tightly and cannot move or slip unless the skull is hit with great force. The skull is balanced on top of the backbone. The spinal cord runs through the backbone and into the brain through a large opening at the base of the skull.

frontal bone forms
the forehead

zygomatic bone
(cheek bone)

infolab

- The bones around the nose are hollow, to keep the skull as light as possible.

- The fontanelles of a baby become bone between 12 and 18 months.

Safety first

Although the skull is strong, sometimes it needs extra help to protect its precious contents. In many sports, such as cycling, skateboarding or American football, it is important to wear protective headgear.

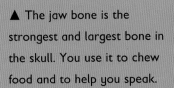

▲ At the front of the skull there are two large openings called orbits. These hold the eyes.

▲ The jaw bone is the strongest and largest bone in the skull. You use it to chew food and to help you speak.

mandible
(lower jaw)

maxilla
(upper jaw)

Fontanelles

In small babies, the bones of the skull have not yet knitted together. Instead, the bones are connected by a stretchy material. The gaps between the bones are called fontanelles. These allow the skull to get bigger as the baby's brain grows.

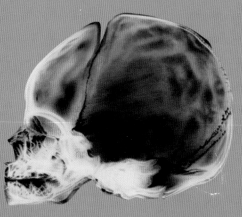

▲ This x-ray of the side of a baby's skull shows the gaps, or fontanelles, that close up as the skull grows.

The face

If you have ever had an injection at the dentist, you will know what happens when the muscles of the face are out of action. You cannot speak clearly and you begin to drool! The facial muscles help you to eat, to speak and to communicate without words.

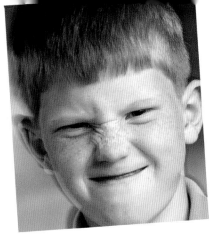

Pulling faces

If you want to know what kind of mood someone is in, just look at his or her face. Facial expressions show others whether we are happy or sad, excited or angry. Many of these expressions, such as a smile, are understood in the same way by people around the world.

▶ The muscles of the face pull on the skin to make all kinds of different expressions, from anger to a look of surprise.

Kissing muscle

A ring of muscle around the mouth pulls your lips into different shapes. This muscle is sometimes called the kissing muscle! We use this muscle to suck, to whistle and to form words when we speak.

◀ When you drink through a straw, a ring of muscles around the mouth goes into action.

frown with
this muscle

wrinkle your
forehead with
this muscle

close your eyelids
with this muscle

smile with
these muscles

the masseter muscle
closes the mouth

when you feel sad,
this muscle pulls
down the corners
of the mouth

the 'kissing' muscle lets
you shape your lips and pout

▲ Facial muscles
are used to express
feelings as well as
to eat and to speak.

▼ A performer from the
1920s demonstrates the power
of the masseter muscle, which
opens and shuts the jaw.

In the blink of an eye

Your eyes have an automatic safety feature. Every time you blink, the eyelids wipe dust and dirt away from the eyes. If any other object gets too close, the same muscles instantly close the eyelid to protect the surface of the eye.

infolab

- There are more than 40 muscles in the face.

- You need most of the muscles in the face to frown, but less than half of them to smile.

- The masseter muscle is the strongest muscle in your body.

▲ ▶ Scientists can re-create the features of a person who lived long ago. First, pegs are added to the skull. These provide an accurate guide for the layer of muscle which goes on next.

Skeleton secrets

After a person has died, the softer parts of the body decompose, or break down. The harder parts, such as bone, may survive for hundreds of years. Scientists can study bones and skeletons to learn how people in the past lived and died.

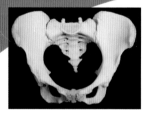

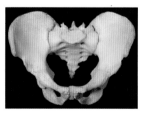

◀ These pictures show a female pelvis (above) and a male pelvis (below). The central opening is wider in women than in men, to allow a baby's head to pass through the pelvis during birth.

All in the bone

Bones provide many clues about a person's health. There may be signs of diseases, such as leprosy or tuberculosis, that are very rare today. Old injuries, from a broken leg to a fractured skull, will also show up. If a broken bone has not healed very well, this may mean that the injury happened not long before the person died.

Back to life

The muscles of the face help to give a person his or her unique features. By moulding facial muscles made from clay on to a skull, scientists can work out how that person looked. This process can now be carried out on a computer.

► This skeleton, nicknamed Lucy, is almost 3.5 million years old. Scientists could tell from her teeth that she was a vegetarian.

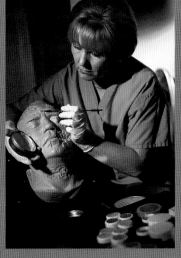

▲ A scientist uses special paints to add the finishing touches to the model of a re-built head.

A girl called Lucy

One of the oldest relatives of humankind was found in Ethiopia in 1974. The skeleton was a female's and it revealed that she belonged to a species, or type, of animal that was more developed than our ape-like ancestors, but not quite human.

▲ The facial muscles are moulded on to the skull with clay. Finally, a layer of clay 'skin' will be placed on top of the muscles to make the person's features even more life-like.

A hole in the head

Ancient skulls from around the world show that holes were sometimes bored into people's heads while they were still alive! This practice, called trepanning, was performed in the belief that it would allow evil spirits to escape.

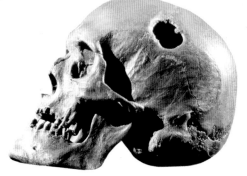

▲ Some ancient peoples believed that mental illness could be cured by drilling holes into the head.

seven cervical
vertebrae in the
neck support
the head

Spine and ribs

Feel the bumps running down the middle of your back. Each one is a ring-like bone called a vertebra. These bones form the spine, or backbone, which is the central part of the skeleton. Twelve pairs of curved rib bones are also attached to the spine.

Support system

The spine is made up of curved sections. Each one has a different job to do, from supporting the head to carrying the weight of your body. The different sections of the spine together form a gentle 'S' shape. This helps to make the spine flexible and strong.

twelve thoracic
vertebrae are
connected to
your ribs

▼ Here, part of a vertebra has broken off in an accident and is pressing against the spinal cord.

five large lumbar
vertebrae carry most
of your body weight

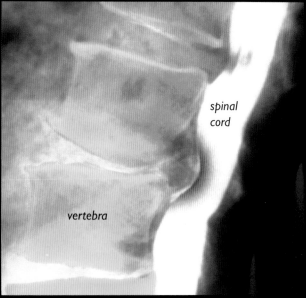

spinal cord

vertebra

these five fused vertebrae form the sacrum, which secures the spine to the pelvis

four fused
vertebrae form
the coccyx, or
tailbone

◀ ▲ The spine has 33 bones – 24 separate vertebrae and nine that are fused together.

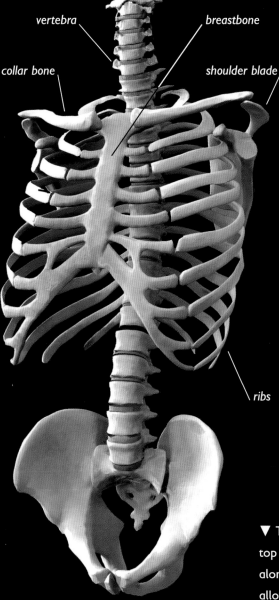

vertebra

breastbone

collar bone

shoulder blade

ribs

▲ The ribs curve around the chest from either side of the spine. Most are connected to the breastbone, or sternum, at the front.

The ribs

The ribs form a protective cage around your lungs and heart. When you breathe, your ribcage moves up and down, helping your lungs to suck in air and squeeze it out again.

▼ The atlas is found at the very top of the spine. This vertebra, along with the one below it, allows you to shake and nod your head.

Anti-shock

When you move, stand or jump, you put pressure on your spine. Between each vertebra there are padded discs of cartilage. These cushion and protect the bones of the spine from damage.

► The atlas, which supports your head, is named after a character from one of the myths of Ancient Greece. This sculpture shows Atlas carrying the Earth on his shoulders.

25

Legs and feet

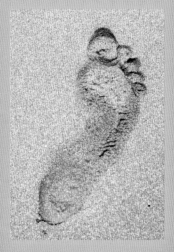

▲ Look at a footprint and you can see that the sole is not flat. Arches of bone raise the inner part of the foot off the ground.

When you are walking, running or just standing still, your legs and feet have to carry the weight of your whole body. The femur, or thigh bone, in the upper part of the leg, is connected to the body by the pelvis. The femur is the largest and strongest bone in the body.

tibia (shin bone)

femur (thigh bone)

Bone basin

The basin-shaped pelvis is where the upper and lower body meet. The pelvis is made from two curved hip bones, joined together at the front. At the back, the hip bones are connected to the backbone.

Under pressure

When you are on the move, your feet push your body forwards. They also stop you from falling over! The bones and ligaments of the foot form curves called arches. These can bend under the weight of the body and they turn the feet into excellent shock absorbers.

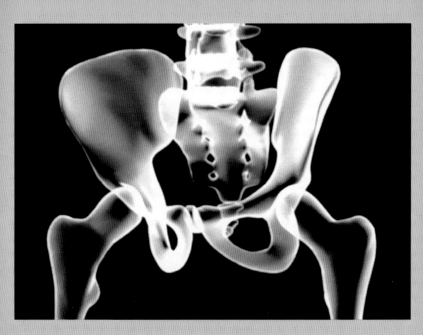

◄ The legs are joined to the spine by the pelvis. The pelvis also surrounds the reproductive and digestive organs.

- There are 26 bones, 33 joints and more than 100 muscles, tendons and ligaments in each foot.

- The muscles of your feet expand slightly during the day.

- The bones and muscles of the arms and legs are very similar.

◄ The bones and muscles in this gymnast's left leg support the body, while his right leg is stretched out.

All in a name

The sartorius muscle is the longest in the body. Found in the thigh, it is about 30cm long and pulls the knee up and rotates the thigh outwards. The sartorius also lets you sit cross-legged. Ancient Roman tailors, called *sartors*, sat like this when they sewed.

sartorius muscle

▲ A triple jumper winces in pain as the Achilles tendon, which connects the calf muscle to the heel, suddenly tears.

tarsals (ankle bones)   *metatarsals* (sole bones)   *phalanges* (toe bones)

► Each foot contains seven tarsals, or ankle bones, five metatarsals, or sole bones, and 14 phalanges, or toe bones.

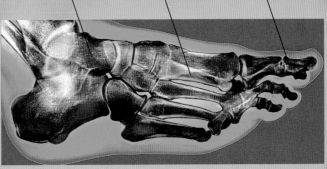

Artificial limbs

▲ This picture shows a 450-year-old artificial hand made of iron. It was designed for people who had lost a hand in battle.

People who have lost a limb because of injury or disease can lead normal lives thanks to artificial replacements. Artificial limbs that use the latest technology can imitate the precise movements of a real hand or foot.

Ancient history

The oldest artificial limb ever discovered was found in a tomb in Italy. It is made from copper and wood and is over 2,300 years old! In the 1400s, many artificial limbs were built by craftsmen who also made suits of armour.

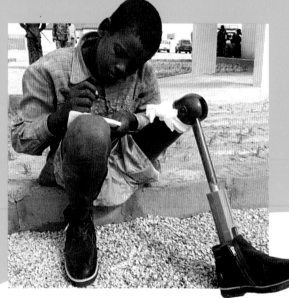

▲ This boy, from the African country of Somalia, lost a leg when a landmine exploded under his foot. There are over 70 million landmines planted in at least 90 countries around the world.

Deadly menace

Every year, thousands of people lose a limb from explosions caused by landmines. These are planted in war zones around the world. Landmines continue to kill and maim people many years after a conflict has ended.

▼ ▶ Some artificial hands are controlled by electrical signals, and have joints that bend. A plastic skin makes them look more life-like.

◀ Tom Whittaker climbed Mount Everest in only three days, using a specially designed artificial foot.

On top of the world

In 1998, Tom Whittaker, who had lost his right foot in an accident 19 years earlier, reached the top of Mount Everest. He was the first person with an artificial limb to climb the world's highest mountain.

◀ Some athletes with artificial limbs can sprint around the track faster than most people with two legs.

Hi-tech marvels

Modern artificial limbs are built from strong, lightweight materials and are comfortable to wear. The latest ones have working joints and computer controls that give a wide range of movements.

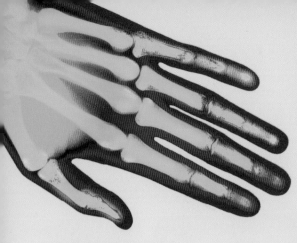

◀ This x-ray shows how the hand bones are arranged. Each finger is made up of three bones called phalanges. The thumb only has two.

▼ Most of the muscles that control the hand are in the forearm. They are connected to the fingers by tendons.

this muscle straightens the fingers

this muscle bends the wrist

Hands

Your hands are one of nature's most amazing tools. From operating complex machinery to catching a ball, our hands are designed to hold and control objects with great accuracy. Each hand has 27 bones and 29 major joints.

Success story

One of the reasons that the human species has been so successful is down to the thumb! The thumb can move across the palm to press against the fingertips. This means that we can perform a huge range of tasks using our hands.

▶ Wrapping the fingers and thumbs around a rope in a game of tug-of-war gives a strong and powerful grip.

Tendons

Every time you make a hand movement, dozens of tiny muscles are at work. Most of these movements are made by muscles in the arm, as there is not enough space in the hand. The muscles pull on long tendons. The ends of these are attached to your fingers.

On the left

Most people are right-handed. But one in nine of us is left-handed. If you are left-handed you may find it difficult to use scissors and other tools designed for right-handed people.

fibres called ligaments hold the tendons in place

tendon from the muscle that straightens the fingers

▲ To play an electronic game you need to make rapid and precise movements with your thumbs.

▼ Special hand shapes and movements are used in sign language. It allows people to communicate without spoken words.

Hand signals

Hands play an important part in human communication – we shake hands, wave goodbye or clap in appreciation. Many people who have problems with their hearing communicate by using special hand movements, called sign language.

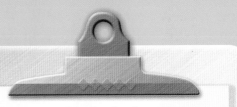

infolab

- In the USA, sign language is the fourth most widely used language.

- In 1989, two million people joined hands to form a human chain across three countries in eastern Europe.

- Each hand contains over 120 ligaments.

The story of a broken bone

Your bones are some of the toughest parts of your body, but they can be broken if they are bent, twisted or receive a very hard knock. Arms are often broken when people fall and stretch their hands out to break the fall. Once a bone is broken it must be fixed back into position.

Fractures

A broken bone is called a fracture. Sometimes the broken bone breaks through the flesh to open a wound in the skin. This is known as a compound fracture and can be very painful. If the skin is not torn, the fracture is called a simple fracture.

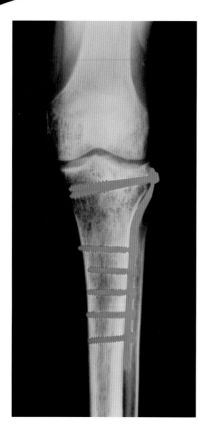

◄ If a bone is broken in several places, screws might be needed to hold the bone together while it heals.

X-ray vision

Doctors check to see if a bone has been broken by taking a special picture called an x-ray. This can see through the skin to the bone itself. Bones are hard and dense, and show up very clearly in an x-ray.

▶ In this x-ray, the two bones below the elbow are broken. At the break, the jagged ends of the bones have moved out of line.

Joining the ends

For a bone to heal properly, the two broken ends must be brought back together. To keep the bones in exactly the right place, the arm or leg is put in a cast. This is a special bandage that turns hard and stops the bone ends from moving.

blood clot

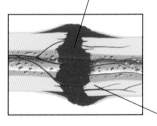

◀ A broken bone heals in several stages. First, a blood clot forms around the two ends of the bone.

broken bone

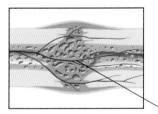

◀ Over the next few weeks, new bone is made and fills the space between the broken ends.

new blood vessels

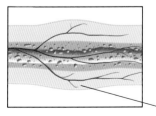

◀ After several months, the bone has healed. It is as strong as it was before the break.

new bone

▶ A plaster bandage, or cast, will set rock hard to hold the girl's broken bones in position.

On the mend

The two ends of the broken bone produce millions of new cells. These cells build up layers of new bone. Eventually, the two ends meet and join up. It can take up to 12 weeks for bones to repair themselves. Once the x-ray has been checked to see that the bone has healed, the cast can be removed.

Get active!

▲ These Chinese children keep fit by exercising every day. Fitness gives you energy, flexibility and strength.

If you want to stay in shape, then you need to make exercise a regular part of your life. From playing football to dancing, exercise strengthens growing muscles and bones. It can also stop you from becoming overweight. And best of all, exercise can be great fun!

Use it or lose it

The more you use a muscle, the stronger it gets. The best kinds of exercise involve moving lots of different muscles. Swimming, cycling and running are ideal for this.

Body fuel

For your body to work properly, it needs healthy foods. You should eat a variety of different foods, including lots of fresh fruit and vegetables. These provide many of the vitamins and minerals that your body needs.

◀ ▶ Exercise is great fun, but some people take sport very seriously. To be one of the best in the world, you need to train for many years and be in peak physical condition.

◀ Swimming gives your heart, lungs and muscles a good workout.

Keeping safe

Get the right kit, or accidents and injuries will spoil your fun. It is important to wear the right sort of protective gear. Helmets are needed for many sports and should fit snugly to protect your head.

▲ For some sports, you need proper protection, such as padding and a helmet.

▶ Many sports injuries can be prevented by doing gentle stretches.

Stretch those legs

Always warm up properly before any sporting activity. This will help prevent damage to your muscles and tendons. Warming up means stretching your body and doing gentle exercise to get the muscles moving.

Glossary

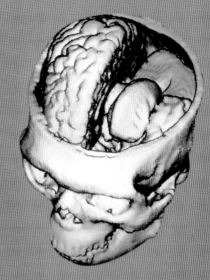

Achilles tendon The tendon that connects the muscle at the back of the lower leg to the heel.

arch The curved shape made by the bones in the foot. The arch lifts part of the foot off the ground, and acts like a shock absorber during movement.

artificial limb A false arm or leg made from wood, metal, plastic and other materials to replace a natural one that has been lost or not formed properly.

blood vessel A tube that carries blood around the body.

bone marrow Soft tissue found in the central cavity of long bones and in spongy bone. Yellow bone marrow stores fat, red bone marrow makes blood cells.

cartilage A tough but flexible tissue that covers the surface of bones in the joints. Cartilage is also found in the nose, ears and elsewhere in the body.

compact bone A very hard type of smooth-looking bone that is made up of bony tubes. It is found in the outer layers of a bone.

cranium The domed upper part of the skull, which forms a protective casing for the brain.

dislocation When two bones next to each other are knocked out of position or line by a very strong force.

fontanelles Gaps between the bones of the skull in a baby. These gaps, which are covered by a stretchy tissue, slowly close up during the first 18 months.

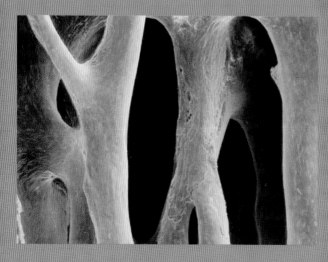

fracture A break or crack in a bone, which may be caused by an accident.

joint A part of the body where two or more bones meet. At most joints, the body can move or bend.

ligament Tough bands of fibre that stretch across or around a joint and hold bones together where they meet.

mandible Also known as the jaw bone, this is the large bone that forms the jaw and contains the lower teeth. It is the only moveable bone in the skull.

pelvis A bowl-shaped ring of bone that is formed by the hip bones and the sacrum. The pelvis protects the organs of reproduction and digestion, and joins the legs to the spine.

skeleton A hard framework made of bones and covered by the muscles. The skeleton supports the body, gives it shape and protects the internal organs.

skull A collection of 22 bones found in the head. The skull contains and protects the brain and gives your face its shape.

spinal cord A thick cord of nervous tissue that runs from the brain down the spine. The spinal cord carries nerve signals between the brain and the body.

spine A column of 33 bones, called vertebrae, that supports the head and provides a path for the spinal cord. Also known as the spinal column or backbone.

spongy bone A lightweight type of bone found in the inner part of bones.

tendon A tough cord of tissue that joins muscle firmly onto bone.

vertebrae Ring-shaped bones that stack on top of each other to form the spinal column, or backbone.

x-ray A type of picture that allows doctors to see inside the body.

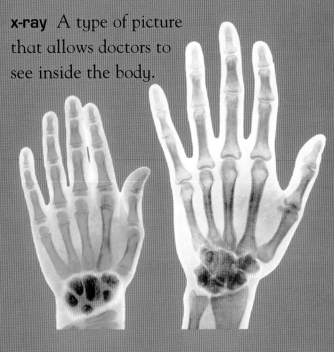

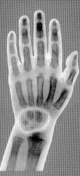

Index

Websites

Kidshealth has lots of information on your muscles: www.kidshealth.org/kid/body/muscles_SW.html
...your bones and joints: www.kidshealth.org/kid/body/bones_SW.html
...and broken bones: www.kidshealth.org/kid/ill_injure/aches/broken_bones.html

You'll find cartoons, quizzes and lots of fun facts to explain how your muscles and bones get you moving at BrainPop: www.brainpop.com/health/

This site, called 'Your Gross and Cool Body', can tell you all about your muscles: http://yucky.kids.discovery.com/flash/body/pg000123.html
...and your skeleton: http://yucky.kids.discovery.com/flash/body/pg000124.html

Play the Muscle Game or the Skeleton Game at BBC Science: www.bbc.co.uk/science/humanbody/body/index.shtml?muscles

Learn about bones with Bud the skeleton: www.usm.maine.edu/gany/bonebuddies/

The Children's Museum of Indianapolis has dozens of fun things to do with bones: http://tcm.childrensmuseum.org/bones/kids_mazeGame.htm

Learn the secrets of the bony remains of people from ancient times: www.pbs.org/wgbh/nova/icemummies/

Acknowledgements

The publisher would like to thank the following for permission to reproduce their material. Every care has been taken to trace copyright holders. However, if there have been unintentional omissions or failure to trace copyright holders, we apologise and will, if informed, endeavour to make corrections in any future edition.

Key: b = bottom, c = centre, l = left, r = right, t = top

Cover l Actionplus; c Science Photo Library (SPL); br Getty Imagebank; page 1 Actionplus; 4 Getty Imagebank; 6tl Actionplus; 6r Actionplus; 6bl Getty Stone; 7l Actionplus; 7tr SPL; 7cr Actionplus; 7br Getty Stone; 8–9 SPL; 10bl SPL; 10c SPL; 10–11 Getty Imagebank; 11r SPL; 12bl SPL; 12–13 Alamy; 13tr Getty Imagebank; 14bl Corbis; 14bc SPL; 14tr Corbis; 15 SPL; 16tl zefa; 16bl SPL; 17br zefa; 18tl Getty Stone; 18bl SPL; 19c Imaging Body; 19cr Imaging Body; 19br SPL; 20bl Corbis; 20r Alamy; 21b Corbis; 22bl Imaging Body; 22t 2003 Tim Gilbert for AIMS Solutions Ltd; 23 SPL; 24–25 SPL; 26tl Alamy; 26b SPL; 26–27 Getty Allsport; 27cr Actionplus; 27br SPL; 28tl SPL; 28cl PA Photos/EPA-UK; 28–29b SPL; 29tl Corbis; 29r Actionplus; 30tl SPL; 30–31 Getty/Photographer's Choice; 31tr Getty Brand X Pictures; 31cl Medical-On-Line; 32 SPL; 33tr SPL; 33cr Corbis; 34tl Corbis; 34bl zefa; 34–35 Corbis; 35t Getty Photographer's Choice; 35c Getty Allsport; 36–37 SPL; poster tl Actionplus; cl Actionplus; c Getty Imagebank; br Alamy